CAMILA CABELLO
CINDERELLA
AN AMAZON ORIGINAL MOVIE

ISBN 978-1-70515-195-2

HAL•LEONARD®
7777 W. BLUEMOUND RD. P.O. BOX 13819 MILWAUKEE, WI 53213

D1126984

Visit Hal Leonard Online at
www.halleonard.com

Contact us:
Hal Leonard
7777 West Bluemound Road
Milwaukee, WI 53213
Email: info@halleonard.com

In Europe, contact:
Hal Leonard Europe Limited
42 Wigmore Street
Marylebone, London, W1U 2RN
Email: info@halleonardeurope.com

In Australia, contact:
Hal Leonard Australia Pty. Ltd.
4 Lentara Court
Cheltenham, Victoria, 3192 Australia
Email: info@halleonard.com.au

RHYTHM NATION / YOU GOTTA BE

RHYTHM NATION
Words and Music by JANET JACKSON,
JAMES HARRIS III and TERRY LEWIS

YOU GOTTA BE
Words and Music by DES'REE
Additional Music by ASHLEY INGRAM

love will save __ the day. __

You got-ta be bad, __ you got-ta be bold, you got-ta, got-ta, got-ta be wis - er. __

SOMEBODY TO LOVE

Words and Music by
FREDDIE MERCURY

Freely

Can an-y-bod-y _____ find _____ me _____

_____ some-bod-y to _____ love?

Moderately

F   C/E   Dm   B♭   C7

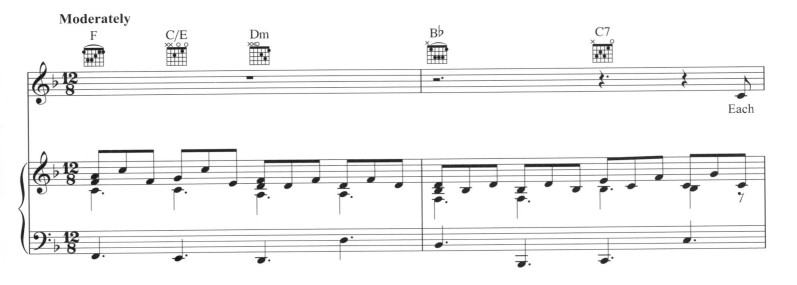

Each

MILLION TO ONE

Words and Music by CAMILA CABELLO
and SCOTT HARRIS

Power Ballad

Here I go a - gain,

I'm i - mag - in - ing a world out - side, un - like the one I'm in.

Day - dream - ing a - gain   of when I'll get a _____ chance.

MATERIAL GIRL

Words and Music by PETER BROWN
and ROBERT RANS

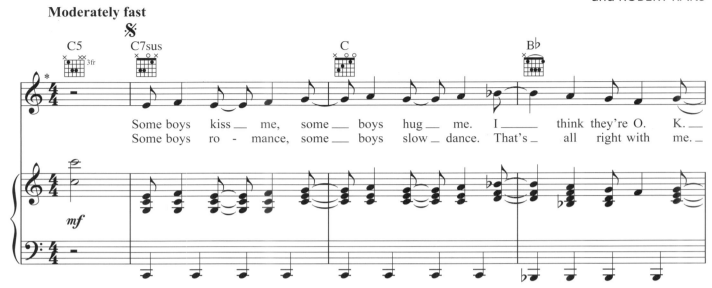

Moderately fast

Some boys kiss__ me, some__ boys hug__ me. I ____ think they're O. K.__
Some boys ro-__ mance, some__ boys slow__ dance. That's__ all right with__ me.__

If they don't give__ me prop-er cred-it, I__
If they can't raise__ my in-t'rest then__ I have__

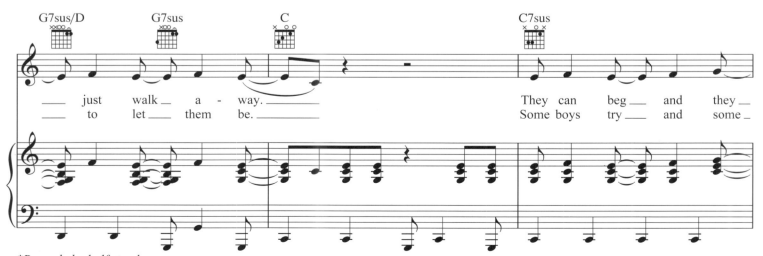

____ just walk a-way.__
____ to let__ them be.__

They can beg__ and they__
Some boys try__ and some__

*Recorded a half step lower.

AM I WRONG

Words and Music by VINCENT DERY,
NICOLAY SEREBA, WILLIAM WIIK LARSEN
and ABDOULIE JALLOW

Moderately, freely

Am I wrong for think-ing out ___ the box from where I ___

___ stay? Am I wrong ___ for

say-ing that ___ I'll choose ___ an-oth-er ___ way? ___ Oh, ___ I ain't

SHINING STAR

Words and Music by MAURICE WHITE,
PHILIP BAILEY and LARRY DUNN

shin-ing star, ___ no mat-ter who you are, _____ shin-ing

bright to see _____ what you could tru - ly be.

Slowly, freely

(Spoken:) Hush now.

WHATTA MAN/
SEVEN NATION ARMY

WHATTA MAN
Words and Music by DAVID B. CRAWFORD,
HERB AZOR and CHERYL JAMES

SEVEN NATION ARMY
Words and Music by
JACK WHITE

Moderately fast

Lyrics:
What a man, what a man, what a man, what a might-y good man. (Got-ta say it a-gain __ now.) What a man, what a man, what a man, what a might-y good man. ___ (Yes he is ___ now.) I'm gon-na

Additional Lyrics

Rap: I want to take a minute or two and give much respect due
To the man that's made a difference in my world.
And although most men are hoes, he flows on the downlow
'Cause I never heard about him with another girl.

But I don't sweat it, because it's just pathetic to let it
Get me involved in that "He said, she said" crowd.
I know there ain't nobody perfect. I give props to those who deserve it.
And believe me, y'all, he's worth it.

Yeah, here's to the future 'cause we've got through the past.
I finally found somebody that can make me laugh.
Ha ha ha, you so crazy.
I think I wanna have your baby.

PERFECT

Words and Music by
ED SHEERAN

DREAM GIRL

Words and Music by IDINA MENZEL
and LAURA VELTZ

Moderately, in 2

I don't care. This is life. It's not fair. It's not

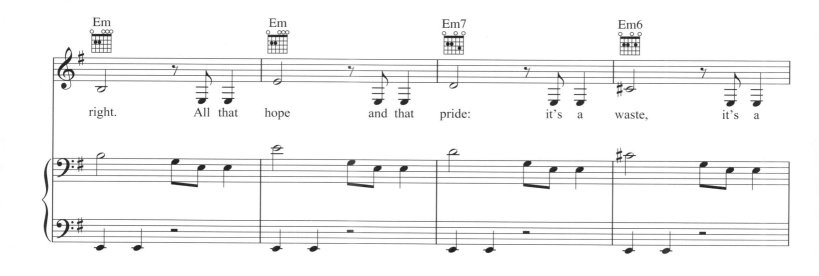

right. All that hope and that pride: it's a waste, it's a

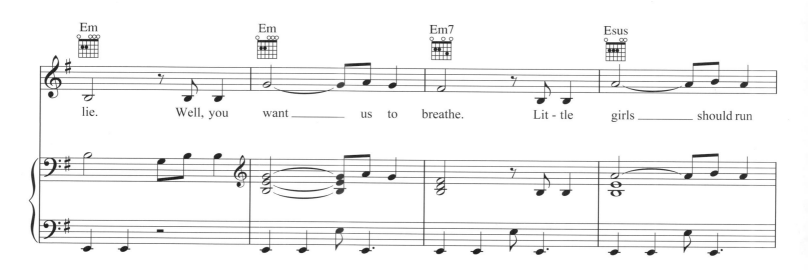

lie. Well, you want _____ us to breathe. Lit- tle girls _____ should run

The world does-n't need an-oth-er dream girl.

MILLION TO ONE/
COULD HAVE BEEN ME
(Reprise)

MILLION TO ONE
Words and Music by CAMILA CABELLO
and SCOTT HARRIS

Half-time Ballad

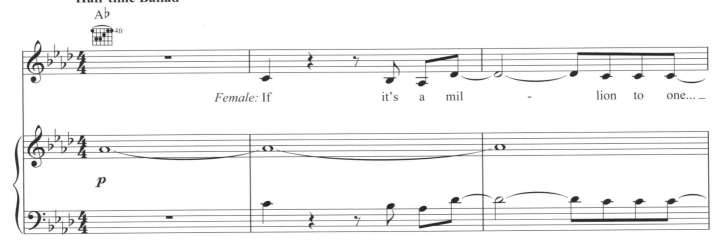

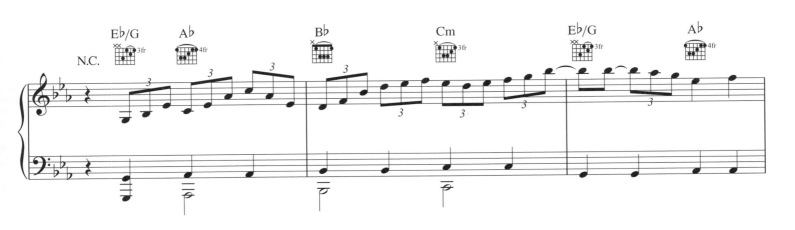

COULD HAVE BEEN ME
Words and Music by ADAM SLACK,
LUKE SPILLER, RICHARD PARKHOUSE,
JOSHUA WILKINSON and GEORGE TIZZARD

Female: If _____ it's a mil - lion to one.

Male: I want to taste

LET'S GET LOUD

Words and Music by GLORIA ESTEFAN
and KIKE SANTANDER

Fm   A♭6   Cm   E♭6   Fm   A♭6

Turn the mu-sic up to hear that sound. _____ Let's get

Cm   E♭6   Fm   A♭   G

loud. _ Let's get loud. _____ Ain't no-bod-y got-ta tell you what

G7   E♭/G   G   N.C.   Gm

you got-ta do, like, "Dat - da - da - da - dat - dat - da." Let's get

A♭maj9   E♭   B♭   A♭maj9   E♭

loud.   Let's   get   loud.